I Love Fall

By Vontavia J. Heard

Dedicated to my mother, my biggest cheerleader.

I love fall!

I love going to the pumpkin patch

And taking pumpkins home to carve

I love when the leaves change colors

And playing in a bed when they fall

I love when it gets cold outside

And sipping on hot chocolate to stay warm

I love harvest festivals

And going on haunted hayrides

I love Halloween

And going trick-or-treating

I love Thanksgiving

And eating leftovers for days

I love going apple picking

And eating homemade apple pies

What do I like about fall?

I love everything, I love it alll!

What do *you* love about fall?

_____

_____

_____

_____

_____

_____

Other Books by Vontavia J. Heard

All Hair is Good Hair

Chasing Butterflies

The Alphabet Book

Everything's NOT Okay

Love, Mr. Hedgehog

The Fibbing Rabbit

A Monster Party

Don't talk to Raccoons

The *Let's Be Bilingual* Series

Made in the USA
Middletown, DE
17 September 2023